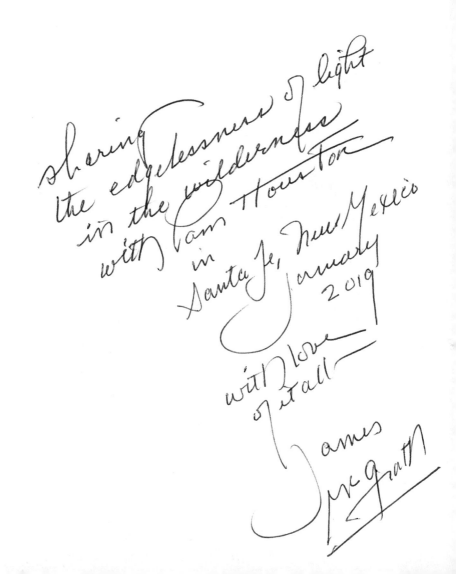

sharing
the edgelessness of light
in the wilderness
with Sam Houston
in
Santa Fe, New Mexico
January
2019

with love
of it all

James
McGrath

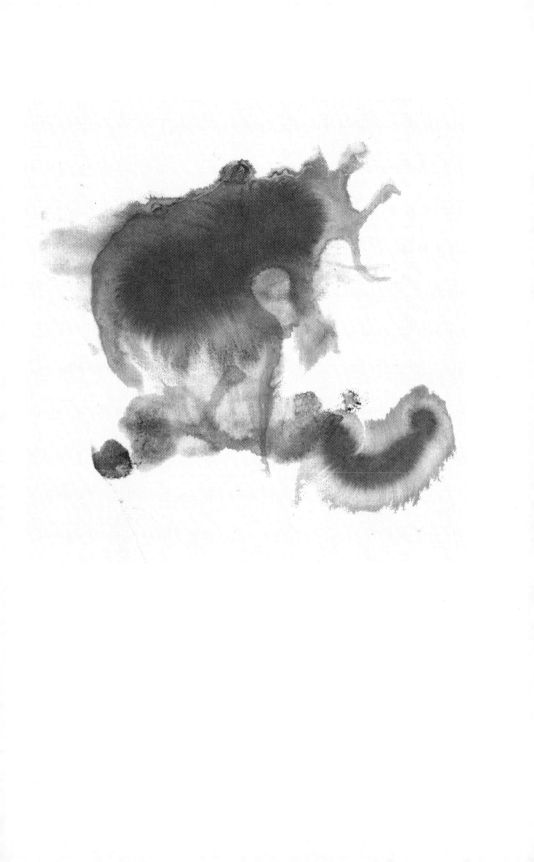

At The Edgelessness of Light

poems   James McGrath

SUNSTONE
PRESS

SANTA FE

Cover: "Shield for the Birth of Clouds," 1969, James McGrath, wax, ink, acrylic, swan feathers, flicker feathers on canvas.
Photograph by Robert Nugent, Santa Fe, New Mexico.

Sunstone books may be purchased for educational, business, or sales promotional use. For information please write: Special Markets Department, Sunstone Press, P.O. Box 2321, Santa Fe, New Mexico 87504-2321.

Library of Congress Cataloging-in-Publication Data:

McGrath, James, 1928-
  At the edgelessness of light : poems / James McGrath.
    p. cm.
  ISBN 0-86534-453-1 (pbk. : alk. paper)
  I. Title.
  PS3613.C497A89 2005
  811'.6—dc22

                                    2005008573

WWW.SUNSTONEPRESS.COM
SUNSTONE PRESS / POST OFFICE BOX 2321 / SANTA FE, NM 87504-2321 /USA
(505) 988-4418 / *ORDERS ONLY* (800) 243-5644 / FAX (505) 988-1025

 DEDICATION

To
those who hear their voices
in the wind,
who see their image
in daily clouds,
who dance about the earth,
one day a raving magpie,
another day a dove.

To
those poet friends
who are willing to speak
their pain and their joys
with words that reveal
life as it is.

To
the memory of those
who have left me
standing in the shadows
at the edgelessnees of light.

Thank you.

ACKNOWLEDGMENTS

My thanks to the publications in which, through the years, my poems have
appeared:

ANTHOLOGIES AND JOURNALS

America Sings, Anthology of College Poetry, National Poetry Association,
    Los Angeles, CA, 1949
Dakotah Territory #6, edited by James White, Winter 1973-74
The Best Man, edited by Sharon Adams, Mandala Publications, 1992
Animals in Poetry, Soulspeak, Sarasota Poetry Theatre Press, 2001
Inside Grief, edited by Line Wise, Wise Press, 2001
Poems by Cancer Patients and Those Who Love Them, edited by Karen
    Miller, Fairview Press, 2001
Unsent Letters, edited by Lauren Smith, Walking Stick Press, 2002
Passager, Poetry Contest Summer Issue 36, 2002, and Fall Issue, 2003
Mercy of Tides, edited by Margot Wizansky, Salt Marsh Pottery Press,
    2003
Hunger Enough: Living Spiritually in a Consumer Society, Pudding House
    Publications, edited by Nita Penfold, 2004
Bardsong, edited by Ann Gilpin, 2004

MAGAZINES

Arizona Highways, August 1976 and January 1978
Perspective, Association for Humanistic Psychology, May 1991
MAN! Magazine, Mandala Publications, Spring 1992
Enkidu, Mandala Publications, Winter 1993

PORTFOLIO

A Crack in the Wall, Baguio Printing & Publishing Co. Inc., Baguio, The
    Philippines, 1981

BOOKS

Language and Art in the Navajo Universe by Gary Witherspoon, University
    of Michigan Press, 1977
Understanding Interpersonal Communication by Richard Weaver, Scott
    Foresman, 1978

The Source, The Image, The Journey, a retrospective of the artist Daryl
    Howard, by Annie Osburn, Eurasia Press, Singapore, 1990
A Warm Stone to Dream Upon, a limited edition of the later work of the artist
    Daryl Howard, by Annie Osburn, Hong Kong, 2004

TELEVISION

Narrative poetry scripts for PBS American Indian Artists Series through
    Station KAET, Arizona State University at Tempe, Arizona, 1972-1975,
    featured artists: *Charles Loloma, Allan Houser, Helen Hardin, R. C. Gorman,
    Fritz Scholder,* and *Lonewolf and Morning Flower.*

My thanks also to the following publications that used my cover design and
    illustrations:

Dakotah Territory # 6, edited by James White, Winter 1973-74
down wind, down river, New and Selected Poems of William Witherup, West
    End Press, 2000

 CONTENTS

What Holds Back the Light

At the Edgelessness of Light

 INTRODUCTION

The title of James McGrath's collection brings another poet to mind: the 17th century Welsh metaphysical poet Henry Vaughan (1622-1695). Vaughan begins one of his verses with these marvelous lines:

I saw Eternity the other night
Like a great ring of pure and endless light.

McGrath is an avatar, a light-bearer, a shape-shifter, a magician. He juggles rings of "pure and endless light." But he is not only *spirit,* he is earthy. Centuries ago he married rocks. He kissed basalt on the Columbia River plateau. He painted antelope, bison, and penguins in the caves of Cosquer and left his handprints on the calcite walls.

It is fitting that he lives now on the site of a former pueblo and kiva outside of Santa Fe, New Mexico. His house is solar-powered; the solar panels follow the sun, tracking the "great rings of pure and endless light." The petroglyphs on the mesa above his house talk to him at night and send him dreams.

It is not my intent here to write the conventional introduction to a collection of poetry. Besides, I would be critiquing a mentor, a teacher who catalyzed my life and charged it with purpose. What I want to emphasize, rather, is that James McGrath is a poet in the original meaning of the word: a maker, a creator, a Guerilla of the Imagination.

McGrath is multi-dexterous. He is a painter, a poet, and a teacher. He does not separate these callings: the poet stimulates the painter, the painter the teacher, the teacher the poet. He told me his first two passions as a youth were *words* and *rocks,* but he had to leave his studies of geology at Central Washington College of Education because of the math requirements. He then studied for an MFA in textiles at University of Washington but took a teaching job out of economic necessity before completing his degree.

His first teaching job happened to be at Columbia High School in Richland, Washington, where I was co-editor of the 1953 school yearbook. McGrath had already discovered one of his vocations: he was a natural teacher, enthusiastic and unconventional.

For several years I tried to organize a *festschrift* for James McGrath, but there were too many loose ends to weave together. And now he has done it himself: given us the gift of a collection of poetry—his textiles, if you will—of burlap, feathers, shells, and small stones.

There is autobiography in these pages, too: parents, uncles, aunts, teachers, lovers, daughters, and grandchildren. One of McGrath's relatives, however, is a dark figure, a shadow who violated his childhood. Afflicted by stuttering as a result of this abuse, the poet overcame it and went on to become a great teacher and arts administrator.

Those who do not paint, sculpt, write, or compose music may not understand, perhaps, the courage it takes to be an artist or a poet. James McGrath has been, for numerous students and friends worldwide, an exemplar of the will and energy it takes to carry the torch of the imagination in a society that values profit over spirit.

Since I began this introduction with the metaphor of "pure and endless light," I will close with a quote from one of my favorite poems in this collection, "Light on Fish Scales." Here are the first three stanzas:

This island light illuminates all shadows.

It arrives from the sea.

At half past five in the morning
when the night lifts its head
to follow the stars,
the light drifts into the shoreline
awakening swans and whelks.

—William Witherup
Seattle, Washington

the edgelessness
of light

In the Edgelessness of Light

Here in the brilliance of this place,
    where light flits from leaf to leaf,
    where light lies resting,
    vibrating on stilts of grass,
    its radiance pulling the shine
    from embarrassed stars,

here where light folds into fading petals
    of wild roses,
    where the feathered light
    of lost geese hovers in cottonwoods,
    its brightness polished by pollen and honey,

here is where I become a shadow in safety,
    retreating,
    leaving shields and spears behind,
    back to the beginning
    where the edgelessness of light
    flares across your face
    and I see you for the first time.

               17 July 2003
               Santa Fe, New Mexico

With A Bowl of Tea
—in memory of Osato-sensei, Tea Master

When I make tea

    for you

I place myself

    in the bowl

and in front of everyone

    I give you

the warm green

    moisture

    of my life.

I shall watch you

    receive

the tea of myself

from the corners of my eyes.

        1 May 1985
        Okinawa, Japan

Poems Among Faded Morning Glories
—in memory of Eleanor Broh-Kahn, my Santa Fe friend

A Poet's words
    get lost among the living.

Hidden in anthologies and files,
    they cry for ears.

In another culture
    we might sing our poems
    on dusty pathways
    or under trees in the shade
    where our conversations
    have meaning and passion.

Now we answer classifieds in magazines:
    "Poems wanted
    with themes of love or grief."

We know how and who to love,
    who to grieve for.

Let us write for one another.
    The words may be held gently
    or be abandoned
    in the silence
    that goes with them
    into one another's ears.

I look out my window this summer afternoon
    to see a dragonfly and the shadow
    of a cat in the faded morning glories.

        1 August 2002
        Santa Fe, New Mexico

I Found a Penny on the Asphalt
—for Betty Taira, my friend

I found a penny on the asphalt.
It had been rubbed
      shiny as a tear
      at the breakfast table,
      bright as anger
      at the dinner table.

I woke up in shadow.
      The taste of night
      lodged against my teeth
      and colored me apricot,
      brown-bruised,
      bruised, brown and warm.

Behind my eyes
      floated sea foam
      and frog cries,
      eucalyptus bouncing
      in masses of holiday ribbons.
I saw kelp beds of lost holidays
      and funerals.

      Nothing wept.
      Stars were breaking open,
      moist with shadows.

I planted orange poppies
      in the shadows,
      knowing they would bud
      on the breasts of waves
      floating to the West
      and their blooms
      would lie in tea bowls
      of rain
      stained with the lips of lichen.

I would like to kiss you
     with my lips
     of huckleberry juice.
We can play spitting games
     with clams.
We will drop pinecones
     into empty wells
     and listen for echoes

18 April 1999
Esalen, Big Sur, California

Ritsos and I

—for Mary Lou Denning, my friend

Like Ritsos,
I want to hold my *briki* pot of coffee
        on top of fragrant dry twigs of thyme.
What coffee that will be!

I want us to row across the night bay of Panteli
        like Argonauts,
        Ritsos pulling on the right oar,
        me pulling on the left.

I'll carry my English-Greek, Greek-English
        dictionary with me.

I'll ask for translations of the moon-waves
        like bits of quartz bouncing on the aquamarine sea.

I'll ask for the words that say *blurp-blurp*
        to both of us
        as we dip our oars.

He will have his moustache running
        across his upper lip
        and along his mouth-edge to his chin.

Out on the waters there will be undulating splashes.

There will be a Greek word for undulating splashes.

I know we will gaze at the moon
        and see nothing,

Ritsos and I.

He will read poems to me in Greek,
        which I will understand
        without knowing a single word,
        like knowing what the moon says.

Ritsos will say,
We've hidden inside each other.
No one will find us.
Only the moon on your
expectant lips . . . *

September 2000
Isle of Leros, Greece

*Iconostasis of Anonymous Saints
by Yannis Ritsos, p. 261
Kedros Publishers, Athens, 1996

Holding Flowers

Perhaps she had no children.
        She holds flowers close to her,
        their pungent smell spiraling,
        leaving a scent of an early wedding.

Oh, she had thought of children
        as women do.
        The fear.
        The bliss.

Together they spoke of the future
        as if planning for something
        no one else would have.

When did the lightning strike them?

It moved in slowly
        without the rumble of thunder.

They were too far away for protection.

When the storm came, it was all fog
        and hazy flashes of blinding light.

Now all she has are flowers:
        her arms are empty except for the dahlias
        and daisies,
        flowers she has planted and she cuts daily
        with her tear-sharpened scissors.

I can't tell you any of her secrets.

If you like, you can wait for her
on your favorite corner
where the children play hide-and-seek
before dark.

She watches from across the street,
waiting for them to be called home.

7 September 2003
Santa Fe, New Mexico

He was a Man Who Loved Oranges

He sat alone
            in a bed of ivy
            peeling oranges,
            his feet hidden
            in the shadows of flying blue jays.

I watched him tear open the film
            of orange skins
            with the sharpness of his eyes.
            Then piece by piece
            he made a mosaic,
            lining his silhouette
            with broken fruit.

He was a man who loved oranges.
The sweet juice ran in his memory.

His eyes were swollen
            with sprouting seeds.

His hands were stained
            and lined with pollen
            that left traces of butterflies
            in his passport.

There were traces of Neroli oil
            behind his ears
            from childhood,
            and when the moon
            went behind clouds
            on lonely nights
            auras of lightning bugs
            circled his head
            and sang songs
            that made oranges blush.

I saw him take another orange,
            press it to his ear,
            listening.

His face showed pain
    as if he heard
    his father calling him.

He tossed the orange
    into the air.
    It floated,
    glistening as the sun
    glistens in fog.

From a pine tree
    a blue jay called,
    swooped,
    speared the orange,
    flew away,
    carrying that orange man's father
    down the cliff-side
    to where sea stones
    were waiting for storms.

That orange man
    jumped from his bed of ivy,
    flew after the jay
    down the cliff-side.

The last I saw of him
    he was breaking open
    the skulls of sea kelp,
    searching
    for his lost orange.

He wanted to have a last word
    with his father
    so he could finish his poem.

                19 April 1999
                Esalen, Big Sur, California

Black Lava Stones

—in memory of James L. White

When you go away
I shall sit among
      the black lava stones
      etched with petroglyphs.

And the birds

      the warriors

      the dancers

      the bears

    the ◎

      the lizards and snakes

      and I shall continue in the myths.

When you return
I shall give the myths to you.

Santa Fe, New Mexico
Published *Dakota Territory* #6, Winter 1973–74:
James L. White, editor

what holds the light

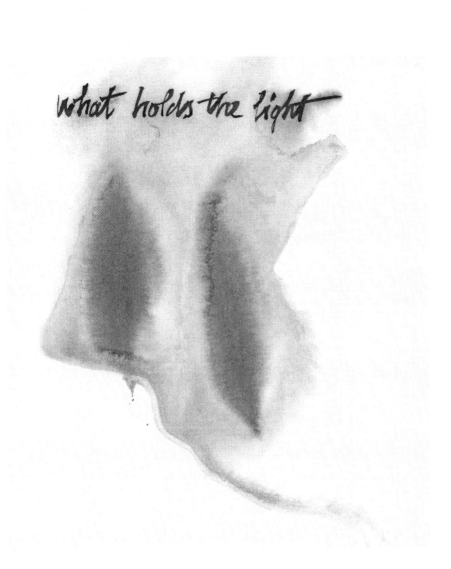

Light on Fish Scales.
—for William Witherup, my poet friend

This island light illuminates all shadows.

It arrives from the sea.

At half-past five in the morning
      when the night lifts its head
      to follow the stars,
      the light drifts into the shoreline,
      awakening swans and whelks.

It pulls the land into itself.

At midday the light massages grey limestone,
      bringing ancient crinoids and bivalves to life
      for people who search for their ancient beginnings.

It is half-past six.
      There is a mouth of white light
      opening and closing
      across the Burren when the sky breathes blue.
      Boastful as the Celts,
      it swallows dark caves and lost sheep.

At night, any hour past eleven,
      when all tides go out,
      the light gasps and sighs,
      guiding fishermen toward the lamp-bright
      windows of their cottages,
      leaving the sweating phosphorescence
      of fish scales in their nets.

          9 June 2001
          Ballyvaughan, County Clare, Ireland

Songs of My Uncle's Horse

—for Martha Yates, my traveling friend

He said,

> a horse is a horse
> only when it is touched.

He said,

> I see the shape of the wind
> when I see my horse run.

He said,

> when my horse is alone
> I see his loneliness go in search of itself.

He said,

> I see the gold in my horse's eyes.
> It is the same gold that lies
> at the tips of water in sunlight.

He said,

> my horse's mane
> is the winter grass blowing.

He said,

> my horse is the dance of time
> when he comes to me.

He said,

> the salty sweat of my horse
> is not bitter;
> it is sweet like the flight of bees.

He said,

> when I ride my horse
> it is without a saddle,
> it is without spurs;
> it is best without clothing of any kind
> so my horse and I
> become the arrow and the bow.

June 1998
Santa Fe, New Mexico
Published 2000: *Animals in Poetry,*
Soulspeak, Sarasota Theatre Press

Aunt Sinnie

—in memory of Uncle Nap and Aunt Sinnie

She spoke to the chickens
    when she fed them
      yellow and orange grain in the morning.

She snorted and gave names to the pigs
    when she slopped them
      with potato peelings, stale bread,
    and sour milk.

She hummed to the chokecherries
    as she made blood-red jam and syrups.

She smiled and winked at the trout
    when they swam near her washtub
    at the edge of the Newaukum River.

Her voice is the memory of wind.

Her face is the shadow under leaves.

Her walk across the porch is the dance
    in the house.

Her eyes shed the raindrops at the end of pine needles.

November 1997
Santa Fe, New Mexico

A Day and a Night at La Union
—for Julius Lee Prater, my friend

This morning
>   just at dawn
>   I followed your footsteps
>   out of the night
>   to the edge of the foam.

I knew they were yours
>   because they
>   entered the sea
>   as the sun came up
>   and disappeared.

I searched all day
>   for your footprints
>   returning from the sea.

Late at night
>   when the moon was full
>   I found them.

I followed your footsteps
>   from the edge of the foam
>   and on
>   under the palm trees.

They disappeared again
>   in a maze of bird tracks.

Did you fly away?

My love is with you,
>   all feathered and soft.

February 1980, La Union, The Philippines
Published 1981: A Crack in the Wall,
James McGrath, Baguio Printing & Publishing Co. Inc.,
Baguio City, The Philippines

Margreta at 90

—for Margreta Overbeck, my artist friend

With pine and cedar
        she grew up in Colorado.

With foxes and squirrels,
        owls and deer,
        she runs with her watercolors,
        enlarging wild eyes and spotted fur.

She flutters the feathers of jays and hawks,
        scratching the papers
        with ink-lines and blurred textures.

She speaks of oil-lamp nights,
        gulping with dolphins and humpbacked whales.

She whirls across fields of bear grass and columbine.

She catches hummingbirds
        as they hover and fill their beaks,
        stealing honey from tiger-striped bees.

                March 2000
                Santa Fe, New Mexico

Maggie at 88

—in memory of Maggie Morse

They say, "Maggie is getting forgetful."

They say, "Maggie doesn't walk much by herself anymore."

Oh! To watch Maggie paint her watercolors.

She fills her paper
        with the iridescent blues
        of Laguna Beach and Hawaii,
        blues that match her eyes
        and her velvet shirts.

She drops the shooting stars of surfers
        into her seas.

She floats sailboats,
        almost too far away to tell that they are boats.

She says, "That's the sailboat I love."

She says, "Those surfers are so beautiful."

I think Maggie forgets
        what she wants to forget.

I think Maggie walks on water
        where sailboats and surfers fly.

I think Maggie doesn't really
        want us to go with her.

                March 2000
                Santa Fe, New Mexico

A Song for Otellie

—in memory of Otellie Loloma

Her hands were clay.

With clay fingers,
    she made portraits of her *miwi,*
    her relatives.

With clay fingers
    she made bowls for her *piki,*
    her blue-corn paper bread.

I think of her pots,
    of the fullness inside
    where the treasures are held,
    secure and loved in their silence.

She gave me her secret,
    her Hopi name, *Sequafnehma,*
    "the place in the valley
    where the squash blossoms bloom."

With her clay fingers,
    she gave me the bowl for the bear.

In the valley of my eye
    I see her now,
    her pollen-covered face
    in the chamisa by the roadside,
    in the last sunflower in my garden.

With her clays,
    she lies under stones
    near Corn Rock
    and dances,
    even now in winter,
    with the broken brown fringes
    in cornfields,
    her clay fingers melting in my tears.

February 1998
Hopi Reservation, Arizona

Collecting Bugs with My Grandson
on a Saturday in Pacific Grove
         —for Dustin Viney, my grandson

They were like small, hard blueberries.

He counted eight of them into his blue
         Ball pint jar.

He had dropped in some blades
         of damp grass and a maple leaf.

The blueberries uncurled
         and became small domed sow bugs,
         little grey-blue pigs with fluttering legs.

He found an earwig under a round,
         black beach-stone.

It hoisted its claw-tail into the air.

He picked it up and dropped it with an *ugh*!

It fell into the grass and was lost.

We saw some grey-brown spiders
         in their white tunnels in the furze hedge,
         deep down in the white beards of their nest.

His mind focused.
         How to reach them?

A stick?
My fingers?

Together we saw
       eyes on stilts,
       looking out at us.

Were they afraid?

For a moment we became two grey-brown spiders,
       caught in our soft, warm home.

He whispered, "I think they are happy there."

            January 1998
            Pacific Grove, California

On the Road to Bhuj

—for Nora Fisher, my India friend

She moves along the road,
       writing her songs to her children
       in the dust.

She carries the forest on her head,
       branches and twigs,
       a bundle of broken dreams.

The bundle of wood on her head
       is a nest for fire,
       for cooking her meals.

At night
       when there are coals in her fire-pit,
       when there are songs of crickets
       and falling stars, and when
       her embroidery is set aside,
       she will retrace her steps to the place
       where she gathered the day's twigs and branches.

She will place a ring of sweet jasmine there
       before she sleeps.

             August 1991
             Bhuj, the Rann of Kutch, India

Just Before Dawn

—for Tom Dickerson, my coyote friend

A time ago
  the eye-curve
  of a new moon and I met in a single
  stream of autumn light
  and we crossed the sky
  with you at our side.

With you at our side we crossed the sky,
  the moon,
  you and I.

The rabbit joined
  us early.
In the rabbit-light
  our trip was warmed.

In the center of the night
  the fox joined us.
In the fox-light
  our trip was quickened.

In the time after
  the fox meeting
  the cry of the coyote
  joined us
  and it speeded our pulse toward dawn.

Just before dawn
  the birds joined us. The moon,
  the rabbit, the fox, the coyote-cry,
  the birds, you and I, all of us together
  entered dawn,
  became a new day.

October 1970, Santa Fe, New Mexico
Published 1972: Dance with Indian Children,
James McGrath, editor, Center for the Arts of Indian America

Men Who Love Windmills

Men who love windmills
    stand on fence posts.

Men who love windmills
    rarely drink water.

Men who love windmills
    have pets in their boyhoods
    like cows or goats.

Men who love windmills
    do not use wrenches to tighten bolts.

Men who love windmills
    love the snap of eating apples in October.

Men who love windmills
    walk by themselves down roads
    and write poems about clouds and wind.

                    October 1999
                    Santa Fe, New Mexico

Blackberry Stains

—for Jennifer Carrasco

I found blackberry stains
on my fingers
late at night.

I thought I saw them
earlier
in the morning
when we were walking
and there was a blush on your face.

August 1972
Santa Fe, New Mexico
Published *Dakota Territory* #6, Winter 1973–4:
James L. White, editor

When Lightning Strikes

Someone is leaning close to me.

We do not touch. We never did.

He was the shadow that shone
        when the lights went out
        and I slept.

He danced around me
        when I waited for the fruit to ripen
        and the bees to gather honey.

He sat at the end of the rowboat,
        dragging his hand in the ripples
        while I rowed,
        afraid to put the boat ashore
        where the sands were warm without footprints.

We were virgin.

We leaned against a hemlock,
        tasting the salty sweat of raindrops
        from alders and cedars.

We painted our faces red with salmonberries.

We spoke of touching
        but thunder tore the sky open
        and a single stroke of lightning
        split the tree between us.

        May 2003
        Santa Fe, New Mexico

Elio Trifio (The Olive Press)
—for Michael and Evangelia Lucas

This year there will be much oil.

Olives are hanging in festoons,
    darkening the earth
    in heavy shadows.

This year there will be singing
    in the groves
    when the olives fall,
    filling old blankets
    and patched cotton bags.

Donkeys and taxis will be needed
    to carry loads
    to the pressing in Temania.

Workers in bare feet,
    their soles softened
    by the oil
    on the floor of the mill,
    will crush and strain
    the heavy blackness away,
    leaving island-green oils
    for cooking *mareetha*
    and steeping tomatoes
    with morning feta.

            19 September 2002
            Isle of Leros, Greece

The Winds of Leros

—for Paige Middaugh, my granddaughter

It was the *mistral*
        or the *meltemi* wind
        that wrinkled and puffed up
        the island for five days.
        I watched it
        tugging like children at olive trees.

It came from the North,
        this wind,
        swirling bougainvillea
        into sculptured coils
        of spiral-shaped hearts in doorways.

The grasping fingers of wind
        loosened the brittle skins
        from roadside eucalyptus trees.

The wind tore the crowing of roosters away
        toward the sea
        and chased hens from their nests.

Afterwards, most amazing of all,
        were the mounds of stones
        along the edge of the beach
        near the *tavernas*.
        Bulldozer tides had dug out
        stones the size of eggs
        and created rumbling cairns
        where only days before
        cats-eye size pebbles
        were playing.

Lazy plastic bags had found refuge,
        tightly grasping wire fences
        or hiding with a clapper
        in the Christos Church bell.

I remember seeing a white cotton glove
        chasing a flash of doves
        out to sea.

                        September 2000
                        Isle of Leros, Greece

Fetish

—in memory of Phillip Patrick Gibbons

I keep it in the second drawer of the *tansu*,
      in the drawer below the Cowichan sweater
      and the *yakata* from Tokyo.

I keep it folded, buttoned, the collar pressed
      tightly against the red woolen chest.

I keep it like a curator,
      like a person who keeps dreams alive
      when dawn comes too early.

It brought me to the eyes
      of a curly-headed pre-med student
      early in my first year of college
      when I was most vulnerable
      to eyes that caught me off-guard.

The first winter, I wore it in a snowdrift
      where we rubbed ears
      to melt the icicles.

I walked in it along spring irrigation ditches.
      We pitched stones at breeding frogs.

Boys who love one another do things like that.

I wore it in a May wheat-field.
      We chewed on the ends of the sweet stems of wheat.

When the school year ended, we embraced,
        promised we would remember our first college year.
        He pressed his dog-nose to my neck.
        He said it was to smell the spring sage,
        summer pine boughs, autumn dust
        and winter bonfire smoke.

He asked me to wear the red shirt as his best man
        when he married.

Boys who love one another do things like that.

                14 December 2001
                Santa Fe, New Mexico

Two Poems for Rio-san

—for Tadao "Rio" Suzuki, my friend in Tokyo

Poem One

Behind my eyes
    I see your face
    smiling
    like tea in a morning cup.

Behind my ears
    I hear your laughter.
    It is the Setagaya-ku shrine bell.
    It is gentle and firm
    and covers my body
    with a *yakata* of sun.

Behind the tips of my fingers
    I touch your cheek,
    your shoulders,
    the tips of your fingers.

Behind all my thoughts of you,
    your poem
    hums on my orange lacquer table.

Poem Two

I shall silently glide away,
      shadowing those cherry blossoms
      blooming late at Ueno,
      holding tight to their paleness
      and nectar.

I shall silently glide away.

Will you remember me?

Please,
      remember me as a cherry blossom at Ueno.

          September 1985
          Okinawa, Japan

Solitude and the Smell of Skunk Cabbage

—for Robert Fearrien, my friend

My solitude was there to crawl into
when the voices stopped and
there was a pause in the sunlight.

One of the best places in the solitude times
might be under the front porch
where there were spider webs,
things dropped between cracks,
treasures covered with dust,
and the upstairs voices were only footsteps
and scrapings of chairs on linoleum.
The porch place was near enough
to be called for dinner or
to answer the question, "Where are you?"

Another good place when there was more time,
like Saturdays and Sundays, was the swamp
and the hill where 48th Street ended.
Three car-bodies made islands in the swamp.
I could jump from one to another
making big tin-drumming sounds
and ripples in the water
that ran across the skunk cabbage leaves.
I liked the middle car-body best.
It was a glorious, warm, blue island on sunny days,
a place to talk to water-skippers
and watch for the eyes of bullfrogs.

Somehow there was so much in the swamp world,
much more than under the porch,
that I never felt alone.
In the spring I could cover the tops
of the car-bodies in pussy willows
and paint my face yellow with cat-tail pollen,
tasting sweet and soft.
The autumn smelled like the world
was slowing down.
Leaves and branches that fell into the swamp
all year were rotting, and sometimes bubbles
floated up to the surface of the water
and *blooped* against a log or just sighed.

In the wintertime there were scatterings of birds:
grouse looking for bugs and crows that talked
like people in the kitchen back home,
and they would sit in their black, bare-
limbed trees and look at me with
orange eyes and ask me questions that
no one else would ask me, and when
I didn't answer they never got mad or
threw a stick. They'd just ask one another
the same questions they'd ask me.
The crows knew all the answers.

> And when I went home
> as it began to get dark
> I'd bring clumps of solitude with me:
> > a smell of skunk cabbage,
> > a bit of swamp-mud-blackness,
> > an orange eye of my own.

June 1992
Santa Fe, New Mexico
Broadside self-published December 1993

Remains

I will not pray for a longer life for my mother.
She is ninety-three with four years of dementia.

She has outlived her two brothers
        and Minnie and Alma.

She has kept the blackberry stains
        on her lips,
            the thorns in her fingers.

She planted her gentleness
        among irises and trilliums
        for seventy years.

She trimmed her camellia bush
        and day after day
        she swept up the tears
        of red petals
        blotting out the sun.

I've kept her scorched-brown cookie-sheets.
        They hold her handprints.

I've kept her piecework quilts
        with the torn edges.
        They warm the bits of childhood I retain.

I've kept the silver wedding coffee-urn
        with the ivory handle,
        the tray, the sugar bowl and creamer.
        They pour out the lady
        that she tries to hold onto.

I've kept the cut-glass pitcher of her mother's,
        sharp-edged and flowered.

I will not pray for a longer life for her.

Her world lies scattered about
in the corners of my home
and on the streets of South Tacoma
where the stones from her garden
paved the potholes of our family life.

I am uncertain what will remain of
my mother when she leaves.

I pray she will go like the camellia petals.

I hope she will carry her secrets away
without leaving any notes
or telephone messages.

Her cat is gone.
The house is sold.
Her earrings wait for the granddaughters.

I will not pray for a longer life for my mother.

I want her to lie full of peace
next to my father
under the dogwood and holly.

I know she will speak her silence
to me
from the fading photographs
in the black embossed albums.

Then it may be time to listen.

December 1997
Santa Fe, New Mexico
Published 2001: *Inside Grief*,
edited by Line Wise, Wise Press,
Incline Village, Nevada

Solitaire

In the back of the house
     where the kitchen bulged out
     into a nook,
     just big enough for our meals,
     Mother kept a square beaded basket,
     holding a deck of cards,
     two Ludwig Drugstore yellow pencils,
     and a brown and blue pencil sharpener,
     shaped like a duck.

She played solitaire,
     listened to the radio:
     Our Gal Sunday,
     Fibber Magee and Mollie,
     Helen Trent,
     Easy Aces.

One spring when I was home from school
     with the chicken-pox
     for almost two weeks,
     I heard the muffled sounds of cards,
     being shuffled in the afternoons.

Even when Fibber Magee opened his closet,
     with the rumble of cascading boxes,
     bottles, shoes and metal objects
     coming from the radio, I could hear
     those sounds of solitaire.

The loneliness of shuffling cards
     entered my room
     and rested on my pillow
     until I went to sleep.

             23 April 2002
             Santa Fe, New Mexico

Nasturtiums and Glue

When I walked into her room
     she was curled into a white ball.

Her gown white.
Her hair white.
Her skin pink, faded nasturtiums.

I whispered, "Mother, are you awake?
     Are you awake?"

She snapped open her pea-pod
     blue eyes. Smiled.

Did she know me?

We went down the hall to the lunchroom.

It smelled stale, like wet crackers.

We sat at a table in the company
     of two other ladies,
     white with nasturtium skin.

The mushroom soup was barely warm.

It tasted like the Lepage's glue
     from Fourth Grade.

          February 2002
          Santa Fe, New Mexico

Before the Night is Turned On
—in memory of Millie May McGrath, my mother

There is no kitchen now,
  no ironing board
  that smells of
  warm cotton.

Yet, she stands there,
  a hissing iron
  in her hand
  and the hum of
  Alice Blue Gown
  billowing
  in the heat-sweetened sheets.

Her hands are
  caressing and folding
  shirt collars
  and tea towels
  with crocheted edges.

She is the warmth
  in the invisible kitchen.

She is the warmth
  left by the softness of
  her hand touching
  my hair
  and tucking
  the flowered quilt
  under my chin
  before the night is turned on.

January 1999
Santa Fe, New Mexico

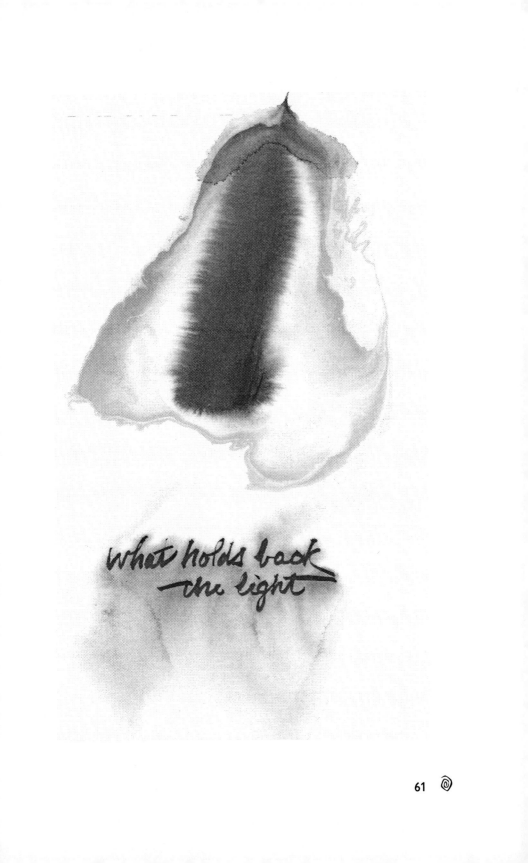

what holds back
the light

The Spaces In Between

He was breathless, his heart
     a bass voice in his throat.

His eyes ached, bled all those
     constellations they had dreamed together.

Ashes of letters greyed the horizon.

He stood, a pillar of salt,
     the car disappearing.

Stones tumbled from the top of the mesa,
     filling the spaces between them.

He thought there is no silence
     emptier than silence without words.
     His words went down the road
     locked in that car.

He thought the planet had stopped beating.

He felt the trees holding tight to their leaves.

Somewhere across the river a dog howled,
     tearing open the space between them.
     They made a pact to howl
     when the moon rises.

He had forgotten that the moon rises every night.

          5 August 2003
          Santa Fe, New Mexico

At Coole Lake

—for Morgan Farley, my poet friend

This stone I lean against is my father's back.

He sits aft in the boat,
    the oars beside us.

The tongue of the lake
    laps against our silence.

Birds at the edge of reeds and hemlocks
    forget we are there.
    They fly across our heads.

We bow and bend.

There are rainbow trout here
    and multicolored feelings
    between my father and me.

I feel them in the quietness
    of this place
    when our backs are one against the other,
    our silence lapping the bottoms of clouds,
    sinking under the waters of this lake.

The poles we hold in our hands,
    his points West,
    mine points East,
    their threaded lines lost
    beneath the surface of all things
    like the lines of our words.

This stone I lean against is impenetrable
    as the days between my father and me:
    dark, hard days.

The surface of this lake,
        like the surface of those days,
        is pitted with an indecipherable language
        that only a son
        may hear from his father,
        indecipherable because there were so few words.

Like the stone that I lean against here,
        there is no pattern.
        There is no edge to this stone
        that may fit it into the shape
        and shadow of the stone
        that sits next to it.

I would like to bring this stone for leaning
        to my home.

It is strong and rough.

The angle of it is comforting.

I can lean back, son-like,
        to hear clouds and time
        flowing from East to West
        like the silence between fishing poles.

This is my silence now.

I am the bait at the end of the fishing-line.

What I catch, I can put back into the waters
        or breathe into a pair of swans.

                        11 June 2001
                        Coole Lake, County Clare, Ireland

When the Movie is Over

What do I do when the movie is out?

>Cross my fingers.
>Cross my heart.
>Hope to die.

No one every questioned me.

>Where I went.
>What I saw.
>Who I was with.

I always had the same answers
>for questions that were asked.

>Cross my fingers.
>Cross my heart.
>Hope to die.

I never knew what I loved most:

>roller-skating on the sidewalk,
>clicking over the cracks,
>alone,
>or
>saving the crusts
>from the peanut butter sandwiches
>for my dog Boy.

Waiting for my parents
        to come home from work,
        I did the dishes,
        brought in the wood,
        sat with Boy and talked,
        wagging our tails.

        Crossing our fingers.
        Crossing our hearts.
        Hoping to die.

                17 August 2003
                Santa Fe, New Mexico

Somewhere Between the Kitchen and the Dining-room

He came into the kitchen usually around 5:30.
He was always led in by the dog
    jumping and wiggling
    and messing up the rugs
    in front of the sink and the stove.

He pulled the bottle out of the narrow cupboard
    where the cutting boards were kept
    and the knife-sharpener.

I stood in the doorway to the dining-room
    where we ate only on special occasions like
    Thanksgiving and Grandmother's birthday.

He never really saw me there.
The dog jumped, and he rubbed his ears
    and spoke muffled dog-talk.

Sometimes he would drink the scotch straight
    with a milk-chaser.
    He would drop bits of plaster and stucco
    on the floor from his overalls,.
    and the dog would rub some chunks
    into the linoleum.

Most of the time his brother John would join
    him in a drink, and they'd tease
    and talk with the dog some more.

I would ease myself through the doorway
          into the dining-room where once, when
          I was ten, Mom made a chocolate cake
          with pennies and nickels in it, and I had
          the Boyle kids in for a party
          with presents and colored balloons
          on strings.

              March 1991
              Santa Fe, New Mexico
              Published 2000: *In Cabin Six, An Anthology of Poetry by Male
                  Survivors of Sexual Abuse,*
              Jill Kuhn, editor; Impact Publishers

Son of the Hunter

—in memory of Francis Anthony McGrath, my father

The deer hung his bronze head.
Dad stood me beside his bronzeness
      like a member of the family.

I let my picture be taken,
      my eyes wandering down his stretched
      hind legs tied with wire to the rafters,

my eyes wandering into the red opening
      that was once a hot stomach,

my eyes meeting the frosted stare
      of deer-eyes browned over
      with the last vision of pine-forest
      and rock-falls.

Even after the camera was put away
      and the hunters left the barn,
      my eyes continued to wander,
      to stop and stare
      at the great silence of coarse fur,
      the wide arching horns.

I wanted to crawl outside my eyes
      to curl up in the open circle
      of those wide horns,
      to be pierced as the deer had been pierced.

I wanted to feel the pain
      of that golden deer.

I wanted to run my teeth against
    the roughness of the horns
    as they entered his head,
    knobby and touched with his blood.

I wanted to be embroidered with his fur
    so I would never be cold again.

I wanted to animal,
    and I wondered how he cried
    when he fell off his mountain,
    and if I put my finger in the bullet-hole
    would he breathe again.

November 1992
Santa Fe, New Mexico
Broadside self-published Fall 1995
Published 2003: *Passager, A Journal
of Remembrance and Discovery*, Mary
Azrael and Kendra Kopelke, editors.

Jumping Salmon

—for Phil McCracken, my artist friend

I was 13.

It was the first time my father asked me to draw a picture:
    a fish on the right side of his new white boat,
    the side that rested against the dock at Steilacoom,
    the side everyone who walked by could see.

He thought a jumping salmon would be nice.

I had never drawn a salmon before,
    let alone one that jumped.

Oh, I had seen them leaping out of Point Defiance Bay
    at the end of his fish-line
    and when he reeled one in near Astoria.

I couldn't just make a silver and black streak
    across the side of his boat
    with a red blur for the mouth
    like I saw them.

I thought about a jumping salmon:
    its body twisting,
    mouth gasping,
    fins stiff, upright,
    tail fanned out.
    A broken circle upon broken circle of water
    erupting.
    The frantic slicing of water from the taut line
    when that fish fled into deeper water.

I looked at labels of canned salmon in the corner store
        on 54th Street: no jumping salmon.

I looked in a book of fishes in the South Tacoma Library
        on my way home from school: no jumping salmon.

I looked in Dad's old copies of *Outdoorsmen Magazine*
        with stories and pictures of men in high-water boots
        on rivers fly-fishing and on cabin-boats
        in the San Juan Islands: no jumping salmon.

That Saturday
        Dad took Mom and me to Ivars By The Sea Restaurant
        in Old Town.
        There on the menu was a jumping salmon
        like a Disney cartoon fish.

Dad said, "There! Like that fish!"

No streaks of silver and black with a red blur for a mouth
        but a fat, smiling, half-moon shaped fish,
        standing on a wide triangle tail
        with a big smile and a winking eye.

It was my first real drawing for my Dad.

He was happy.

                May 2002
                Santa Fe, New Mexico

Yes!

I wasn't there.

I don't know the last thing my father said of me.

Did he speak of his only son?

Did he ask about his son living so far away
    in New Mexico; would the boy come home
    before he died?

Did he worry about where his guns
    would go after he died; would the rifles
    ever be used again to kill a deer or elk?

He didn't admit his son had left him
    so many years before, pushed away.

This isn't the whole story.

The fact is, I was too busy staying away
    from the emptiness to flush out the story.

From fragments of the what and where and who,
    I suspect he brought my name up
    and wondered about my whereabouts.

Perhaps he was making certain that the hunting dogs
    had a home, that my mother knew the house
    was paid for, the insurance on the car
    was in good order.

He was a practical man. He took care of things.
   He was honest and generous.

After he died, Mother asked me if I wanted his guns.

I knew she would.
I said Yes.

> 7 June 2003
> Santa Fe, New Mexico

Echoes in the Storeroom

Some voices never go away,
      like fathers' and dogs'.

When I speak of what I remember
      my father told me,
      I hear him in the distance,
      speaking of carrying the gun properly,
      his dog with us, panting softly,
      speaking with ears erect, tail wagging,
      the three us alert to the splitting
      of pine needles
      as we walked in the forest
      in those Autumn hunting days.

His guns now stand upright in a closet,
      specially built, in my storeroom
      behind the books.

What will I finally do with their cold steel echoes?

Perhaps I will seal them into the wall
      when I re-plaster that room.

Then, when a stray dog comes to my backdoor,
      we will have other things to talk about.

               13 September 2003
               Santa Fe, New Mexico

Filling in the Spaces

I have hidden from eyes
    that believe they are mirrors,
    who read me like tea leaves
    or tracks in dust.

Did you know that I kept my eyes open
    through all the tremors and sighs
    of our love-making?

I believe you knew those tremors
    better than I did.
    You never said a word
    until I finally left.

I think you knew the lava was bubbling.
    Expecting the earthquake,
    you let me go into the streets
    to paint the shadows:
        bleeding red poppies
        black-eyed olives
        pus-yellow.

It is too late for me to return.
    You went to bed before
    I could unlatch the screen
    to knock faintly
    on your stained-glass door.

I could never have awakened you.

Today, even in winter,
    I sit in my orchard
    scratching passwords
    on the bark of apple trees
    in a language you never understood.

        October 2002
        Santa Fe, New Mexico

The Sharing of Silence
—in memory of Jean

Yours is the hot silence that floats
    down the hillside
    in the early afternoon
    with the closing of morning glories.

It lies in all the faded photographs
    that hold your face.

Your stillness is under my feet
    where your footsteps are covered with dust
    and the echoes of falling rocks.

We should have carved our names in the tree
    by the river
    to grow old together
    but the bark of the cottonwood
    was too rough for carving.

Instead we sat mute
    in the shade of that big tree,
    aging alone in our silence,
    deepening the shadows.

        20 August 2002
        Santa Fe, New Mexico

Listening to Stones

—in memory of Toni Drees

I hear the wind
>the way stones hear
>the wind.

I hear quail whirring
>to the mesa top
>the way stones hear
>the quail.

I hear clouds dragging
>their shadows along the hillside
>the way stones hear
>shadows.

I hear the dropping
>of juniper berries in October
>the way stones hear
>falling berries.

I hear the tearing
>of cottonwood leaves
>from their branches
>the way stones hear
>the crying of autumn leaves.

I hear the memory
>of falling rain
>after the rain has fallen
>the way stones hear
>rain.

I hear the stones more than I hear myself.

>8 September 1999
>Santa Fe, New Mexico

When No One Was Listening

All through my school years I stuttered;
     from kindergarten through college
     I stuttered.

He told me never to tell anyone
     what he did to me.
He told me never to say anything

So I hid in silence.
     In school I would whisper.
     Somehow, I could whisper.

I often got caught
     and spent many days in the cloakroom,
     that awful creosote-smelling cloakroom
     with galoshes and lunch sacks
     and damp woolen scarves.

I wrote a lot of notes to Jackie and Coral and Dick.
They were intercepted by those teachers
     in tight-fitting jersey dresses
     who sent messages home to say
     Jimmy must pay more attention in class.

Once in high school I wrote a poem that
     Mrs. Cunningham asked me, out loud,
     if she could read to the class.
I nodded, yes.
She must have decided that I couldn't
     read my own poem.
That poem was in Grade Eleven.
She never knew I had boxes of my voice
     from Grade One, Grade Two, Three,
     Four, Five, Six, Seven, 8, 9, and 10.

Even when Uncle Fred died,
    I still stuttered and kept silent
    and wrote poems.

I stopped stuttering that day
when my poem greeted me and said,
"I love you,"
    and no one was listening.

February 1999
Santa Fe, New Mexico
Published 2000: *In Cabin Six, An Anthology
of Poetry by Male Survivors of Sexual Abuse*,
Jill Kuhn, editor, Impact Publishing

When I Came Home From School

When I came home from school
    he would be there
    lying in the darkened room
    where the wallpaper
    held pink blooming roses
    with broken stems of thorns.

He called me into his darkness
    even before the screen-door
    slammed shut.

I held my breath
    stopped breathing
    stole the darkness and smells
    of his room
    stuffed that darkness inside myself
    while he unbuttoned my clothes
    made me naked
    tongued me
    and made that dark room
    roll with flashes
    of colored stars and thorns.

April 1990
Santa Fe, New Mexico
Published 2000: In Cabin Six, An Anthology
of Poetry by Male Survivors of Sexual Abuse,
Jill Kuhn, editor, Impact Publishing

The Poet as Prisoner-of-War: Four Poems
—for Frances Hunter, my poet friend

Poem One

I put white paper doilies
    around the legs
    of all my words.

Not to soften them
    but to make them crisp,
    bright with meaning.

My inquisitors tore at my words,
    shredded their beauty,
    dulled their sharpness.

I should have put my images
    in rusted leg irons
    and rubbed them across the chalkboards
    of their teeth.

But my poet came out.
    I only wanted my words
    to love them.

Poem Two

Each night now
    the giant eye of the white guard-light
    forces
    the phantom arms of the tree
    outside my small ribbed window
    into a web
    across the floor of my room.

It twists
    among the iron coils of my broken bed,
    wiring me tightly
    to the chill of the room,
    binding me,
    suffocating me in my bandages.

Last night
    I dreamed
    I was in blackened swaddling clothes
    in a manger,
    I, the soldier.

Poem Three

The white shield of myself
     is wounded,
     blood-splattered,
     soaked in sweat
     not my own,
     ripped with pain,
     fired with screams
     at night.

I pull the sand-caked khaki blanket
     over my head
     and weep
     and weep.

Poem Four

For three nights
        a ghost came to my room
        all covered with words
        and bits of sentences.

She said,
        "Take a word,
        any word."

I reached out,
        took SPRING.

She screamed.
        "Take another!"

I took CHILD.

She laughed.
        "Another."

I took PEACE.

She disappeared.

I spit on these three words
        and rub them into my chest.

I make a tattoo.

In the morning
        they come.

They put me in a line
        against a freshly white-washed wall.

They use my chest as their target.

Tonight I shall visit their rooms,
        demanding that they take
        a word from my body.

They will have small choice.

                    January 1991
                    Santa Fe, New Mexico
                    During the Gulf War
                    Broadside self-published January 1991

I Shall Write Your Name in Bullets

The medics cannot find my wounds.
They find only my blood.
They do not see my heart.
Tomorrow I shall leave this field of war,
       this field, this desert place
         where I have reached out through my tent at night
         to arrange stars into the image of you.

Your image is arranged in the blackness.
I listen to screams of desert foxes mating,
       I shake in the beads of sweat
       that wanting gives.
       I hear the cry of foxes in heat
       echoing in my home valley.

I try to wail. I stroke myself.
I soak my stiffened blanket with my sweating,
       and the night is heated and burnt to coal
       as your image in the stars fades.

Again in the morning you come by my tent,
       you, dressed in the black *shashaft*,
       its hem smoothing the sand into a bed for lying on.
Your footprints make a quilt pattern
       for my nakedness.

I never see your face or neck.
I never see your breasts or stomach.
I never see your thighs.
I cannot smooth out your mound of soft, sweet hair.
I cannot read the message of your legs or ankles.

I will never see you now.
I will never speak with you,
        cupping your voice to my ears.
I will never see my face reflected in your eyes
        or feel my body next to yours.

I will never spread honey on your shadow.
I will never surround you with a cloud of myrrh and cardamom.
For ages you have passed my tent at dawn.

Who are you? Leave your name for me at the gate
        and I shall write your name in bullets
        in the dunes of the Neutral Zone.

I will carry your long black shadow behind me forever.
And my wounds, oh, my wounds.
The medics cannot find my wounds.
They only find pools of my blood soaking the sands.
They cannot see my heart.

Before I leave, I shall drown myself in the mirage
        at your feet, and we shall spend our Arabian nights
        together, wrapped in barbed wire.

                    October 1991
                    Written during the Gulf War
                    after leaving Sana'a, Yemen

Out of the Earth

When she knocked at my door,
    I thought, "Who found their way down the road?"

I opened the door.

"James, it's Malika
    from Basra. May I come in?"

A black coffee later, she spoke of the air raids
    and the killing in her village.

How she hid with the children
    under the garbage in the ditch
    beside her home.

How they crawled down that ditch in the dark
    until they reached the river.

How they found the dugout the family had hidden.

How the children crawled into the bottom of the boat.

How she covered them with river grasses,
    waded into the river, pushing the boat slowly,
    how she climbed in when she felt the current
    catch her body.

How they drifted a full day, passed burning villages,
    bloated bodies passing them,
    eddying around their boat.

How they avoided being beached at night.

How they feared the rapids.

She spoke as if she came right out of the earth.

                    26 December 2002
                    Santa Fe, New Mexico
                    Written during the threat of the Iraq War

Rachel Corrie: *Yakhti*

She was alone
>with the world around her
>in its black screaming coat.

Even the stars held back.

She stood alone
>showing her passport
>to the mask of death,
>grinning, staring.

The sun drew clouds over its face.

She stood silent
>in the rubble of torn *habara*
>and *galibayya*, broken pots of *felafel*.

The steel mouth of the bulldozer ate her whole.

>19 March 2003
>Santa Fe, New Mexico

Yakhti: my sister
habara: woman's traditional headscarf
galibayya: man's traditional dress
felafel: balls of ground beans or chickpeas

Thirty Thousand Food Packets

Thirty thousand food packets,
      wrapped in silver foil,
      are dropped in the hungry fields
      outside the bombed, lightless city.

They fall in the fields planted with mines.

We can hear explosions during the black hours
      after midnight.

In the morning,
      eighteen hundred elders and orphans,
      some in rags, some with crutches or canes,
      some deaf or almost blind,
      volunteer to gather the waiting packets.

They leave at dawn.

We can see the blinking silver in the fields.

We can hear new explosions during the dusty hours
      of morning light.

                4 October 2001
                Santa Fe, New Mexico
                During the Afghanistan War

Collateral Damage

My grandchildren are having nightmares.

After school,
> they sit in front of CNN and NBC
> looking at their classmates on buses torn apart,
> their faces smashed by broken windows,
> their screams burning with flaming tires.

At night, my grandchildren's sleeping sobs
> waken the dogs that whimper beside them.

On Saturdays,
> they visit neighbors watching the children of Basra
> huddle in the corners of their ruined mud homes,
> the bodies of their mothers smothering them,
> the limbs of their fathers in the garden
> mingled with torn donkeys and broken carts.

At night, they hear the crashing of their bedroom walls
> and rush into the room of their parents
> to shake them awake.

On Sundays,
> before school the next day,
> they hear TV preachers calling Islamic people
> godless murderers.
> They hear an American president speaking of evil
> empires and telling them to pledge allegiance
> to the flag under God
> while a bomber with their country's flag on its wings
> drops death on a wedding party.

At night, my grandchildren shriek in their sleep,
    wetting their beds.

At school, they learn to pronounce COLLATERAL DAMAGE,
    looking into mirrors.

                    17 July 2002
                    Santa Fe, New Mexico
                    During the Iraq War

Speaking with Magpies
—for Joe Moore, my long-time neighbor

Out here I can say anything
        among the frozen apples
        and bird-pitted pears.

There is no one to hear me;
        yet if I tell a lie,
        the trees will crowd in
        to rub their bark against my tongue.

I watch the windmill in the field
        roll in its circling about the earth,
        pulling up the waters
        for magpies and me.

We speak,
        the magpies and I.

We speak of what is important:
        black and white feathers
        persimmon eyes
        night
        twigs for nests.

We continue to speak:
        leaf mulch
        open gates
        dried grasses
        shadows of clouds.

We will go to the mall,
        the magpies and I.
        We will speak with radiated tomatoes
        and beef-marrow bones.

                October 2001
                Santa Fe, New Mexico
                Published 2004 in *Hungering Enough*:
                Living Spiritually in a Consumer Society,
                Nita Penfold, editor, Pudding House Publications

There is a River Running in the Blood of Him

There is a river running in the blood of him
    as he tumbles down the mountainside,
    rolling the stones aside,
    scattering birds.

A river running in the blood of him
    tosses his arms with the reeds and rushes
    in the greenest of thunders
    and the gold dust of rain.

A river running in the blood of him
    murmurs and purrs
    when he sleeps
    where he sleeps
    in the distant places without names.

Oh, the sound.
Oh, the whimper of a river running in the blood of him,
    frog voices dark,
    escaping as the moon rises
    on a coyote's wail.

Oh, the fury.
The river running in the blood of him
    calling for a response
    from the sun setting
    too early in his daylight.

Only the newest of moons can cup
    and hold the tears
    running in the blood of him.

September 2000
Santa Fe, New Mexico
Published 2001: *The Cancer Poetry Project,*
Poems by Cancer Patients and Those Who Love Them,
edited by Karin B. Miller, Fairview Press

at the
edgelessness
of light

On the Wall Above the Sea
—for Jeni Keleen Viney, my poet daughter

I am leaving my stone in the Burren
    on the wall above the sea.
    Each day the wall is taller.

One day, when it is tall enough
    and it shoulders the clouds in the night,
    I shall reach up
    to take the stars in my hands.

I shall be pulled up
    to become the light that shines
    from all the nights in my life.

I shall erupt with the lark
    to let the bees sting the final poem
    from my fingers.

June 1997
Ballyvaughan, County Clare, Ireland
Published 2003: *Mercy of Tides, Poems for a Beach House*,
Salt Marsh Pottery Press, Margot Wizansky, editor

The Lichens on Yeats' Tower
—for Susan McDevitt, my poet friend

You say they are only white lichens on the walls.

I see unfinished frescos,
      unfinished paintings torn from time
      bit by bit,
      white now
      in the spring when swans drop feathered arms
      for shelter,
      when the mirrors of water
      rustle the trees on their banks.

You say lichens are ancient plants
      that live on air
      and the little that their stones
      can give away.

I see maps of invisible places
      that the moon has splattered and dripped.

I see fragments of lost faces
      that rushed by on trains,
      that cried in crowds.

I see the birthplace of clouds.

You say these lichens discolor
      and hide history.
      They need to be scrubbed away.

I see them as a language
       words do not speak,
       that shadows betray,
       that tides leave behind during the night.

Please, say no more.

Put your finger on one lichen.

You will feel yourself
       when you blossomed for the first time.

June 2001
Yeats' Tower, County Clare, Ireland
Published 2004: *Bardsong, the Journal for Celebrating
the Celtic Spirit;* Midwinter Issue, Ann Gilpin, Editor

Spring-cleaning

—for Yvonne Schack, my friend of many years

Begin again.
Light the fire.
Throw all books and hiking shoes
    and patch-worked dreams
    into the flames.
Add the layers of family blankets,
    the collection of butterflies.
Make oils for burning of old photographs,
    the scratched 78s of Frank Sinatra
    and the dead flies from window sills.

Begin again.
Don't look into the cardboard boxes
    with their flaps folded in on one another.
Just drop them heavily into the flames
    and step back.
Some will throw sparks.
Some will sizzle and smell bad.

Empty the desk drawers
    of postcards,
    foreign postage stamps,
    the lists of people met
    and lost on trains and boats.

Then late one night
    when the ashes have cooled,
    step outside.
Walk under the Big Dipper.
Put your face up.
Close your eyes.
Let the dipper pour its waters over you,
    stripping away your clothes
    and your skin.

Stand naked.
Your muscles tight.
Your blood chilled.
Your feet planted.
Your bones transparent, and begin again.

Walk East.
Meet the sun.
Look at your new clothes.
Open your mouth.
Listen for the first line of your new poem
        and begin again.
Speak your first line for the first time.

January 1998
Santa Fe, New Mexico
Published 2002: Poetry Contest Winner: *Passager*,
Mary Azrael and Kendra Kopelke, editors.

If Ghosts Could Speak

—for Betty Rosenthal, my friend

I go down my road
      with everything that I love
      walking beside me.

My feet mark the packed brown dirt.

I take in the lightness
      of trees changing colors.

I meander through stones and weeds
      on the islands between the two rutted pathways
      left by trucks and cars,
      cows and horses.

There are ghosts here
      that crowd up and down
      on my road.

They walk just above the earth,
      leaving no prints.

The wind blows through them.

They keep the roadway clear,
      except for dust-devils
      and shadows
      and rocks trying to escape
      their silence.

Weeds crowd the edge,
　　　　pushing to get glimpses
　　　　of the ghosts of horses and foxes,
　　　　barefooted women and bent men.

If the ghosts could speak,
　　　　they would twist birdsongs
　　　　into ribbons of melancholy
　　　　and endless red dawns.

If the ghosts could leave this roadway,
　　　　they would set the apples free,
　　　　pull quills from the porcupines
　　　　and make long capes of cottonwood fluff.

One day
　　　　I will join these ghosts on my road.

I will rest against a tree
　　　　in my orchard in the Spring.

I will drink jimsonweed tea
　　　　and fly off to the stars,
　　　　escaping the long winter nights
　　　　when this road
　　　　pulls a blanket of ghosts in on itself.

　　　　　　　September 1999
　　　　　　　Santa Fe, New Mexico

Self-portrait

—for Jain Kelain Middaugh, my daughter

In a college painting class
      I used palette knife and hot orange
      and blue oils on burlap.
      Then I was rougher, bolder,
      and more open,
      woven like burlap.

Now I am more grey and fading sunset darker.

During my fifteen years with the Indians
      I painted my portrait
      on a round canvas shield.
      It was full of feathers and bird tracks,
      and the back of the shield
      was tightly tied with rawhide thongs
      like a drum.

Now I am more loosely fitted,
      my edges even,
      more rounded and smoothed,
      gentler like a glacial pebble.

In the Middle East I carved my portrait
      in a green stone in Yemen.
      It was the Arabic word for cloud.

I am closer now to that cloud sculpture.
I am feeling my shadow more clearly,
        and if I do create another self-portrait,
        it will be drawn
        in the sand on some warm beach
        as the tide comes in,
        so it can be erased,
        and I can walk away from it,
        smiling.

            September 1998
            Santa Fe, New Mexico
            Published 2002: Poetry Contest Winner: *Passager*,
            Mary Azrael and Kendra Kopelke, editors

Vernaccia Di Sardegna
         —in memory of Jennie Lea

I met Paolo Contini at Cabras
         near the remnants of a floor
         of broken Phoenician tiles
         picturing blue, green, red
         wine-drinking.

The Continis made Vernaccia.

They kept bottles
         in the cool, dusty
         back room of the beach house.

At dusk Paolo caught a small octopus.

It was roasting on coals
         in the fireplace.
         Artichokes were sizzling
         in olive oil and herbs.

We were drinking the sunset
         in small glass jars.

Hours flew off with the fading light.

Our faces were lit only by
         the burning eyes of night birds:
         a petrified owl on the edge of the roof,
         frozen sea birds near the sliding
         in-and-out of the busybody surf,
         and small brown birds kept awake
         by light breezes scattering
         pink flowers in the almond trees.

If the moon had overtaken us,
         we would have gone blind.

                    5 April 2003
                    Santa Fe, New Mexico

Secrets in the Mountain

—for Julie Reid, my friend

In my winter months,
    I go to the mountain,
    joining crags and tree stumps
    to listen for echoes
    left behind in the tracks of deer.

I have left secrets there
    made of ashes
    no one could whisper but me.

I hear quail whirling to the ridges,
    clouds dragging their shadows
    along cliffs.

I hear the wailing of cottonwoods
    as their last leaves stumble
    into beds of scree.

If I listen with the ears of pinecones,
    I hear brittle lava songs
    that rattle like obsidian flakes
    on the belts of raccoons and skunks.

You are the last secret I shared
    with the mountain,
    the swallowed tears
    I slipped under glaciers.

        December 2003
        Santa Fe, New Mexico

The Forest Holds My Words

When I bleed on my paper,
       the sky catches, holds my blood.

Trees become my veins
       and I flow between stones
       into rivers that race to the place
       where I was born.

There are red fish swimming in my veins.
There are red shadows waiting in my veins.

When the sun finally sets
       and the night whispers my name,
       then the forest holds my words
       and I sleep comforted by what I love most.

November 2003
Santa Fe, New Mexico
Published 2004: *A Warm Stone to Dream Upon*,
Annie Osburn, Hong Kong

What Can I Leave Behind?
—for Annie Osburn, my friend

If this is the last time I am in this place,
    what can I leave behind?

Perhaps better that I ask what I can take away,
    without leaving a space in the foliage.

I wish to steal the gold that lies on Panteli Bay
    at sunset.

I wish to steal the long, sharp calls of morning roosters
    and the gentle boiling coffee in my *briki* pot.

And for touching, I will take the sunrise warmth
    of your cheek when we meet near the tamarisk.

And this is what I will leave behind: my imprint on your cheek
    that we each may survive the broken night.

        23 September 2002
        Santa Fe, New Mexico

The Meeting Place
—for Daryl Howard, my friend

To see you
        is to imagine
        someone I have met for the first time.

There is light in the meeting:
        a radiance that calls out
        when the heart breathes,
        when the darkness vanishes.

In that fading mystery
        is the pause at the center,
        spiraling
        between moonlight and dawn,
        the place midway,
        that separates us.

The brightness of light has no words,
        as shadows have.
        It is the shadow that has edges.

Oh yes, I can turn trees and stones
        into suns with my words,
        cross out rivers that flood,
        put fear into jars.

Let me begin by breaking off pieces
        of the poem I write to you with shadows:
        not the words,
        the feelings,
        those spaces between you and me
        where I tell the truth,
        where I die.

                11 July 2003
                Santa Fe, New Mexico

At the Edgelessness of Light

—in memory of Paulette Beall

I have spoken enough of darkness:
  early years playing hopscotch
  with a single piece of broken glass
  without a playmate, playing
  hide-and-seek
  with a growing crowd of sharp-eyed ravens.

With a room full of paint and brushes,
  ink and canvas, stone and chisels,
  I built mountains close enough to the sky
  that I could throw new stars
  into constellations others named
  "Coming Home" and "Maps to the Future."

As the darkness filled more and more
  with clues to how things happen,
  winters became shorter,
  shadows thinner,
  harsh words softer,
  and chinks in the wall became
  undulating crosshatches of edgeless light.

Sorry. I began to speak to you about light.

It is just that I wanted you to know
  about the remnants of darkness first,
  before I go blind
  and the moon sucks me up.

    17 July 2003
    Santa Fe, New Mexico

PSIA information can be obtained
www.ICGtesting.com
nted in the USA
DW02n0059061017
44FS